Best Easy Day Hikes
Yellowstone National Park

Best Easy Day Hikes Yellowstone National Park

Fourth Edition

Bill Schneider

FALCONGUIDES

GUILFORD, CONNECTICUT

FALCONGUIDES®

An imprint of The Rowman & Littlefield Publishing Group, Inc.
4501 Forbes Blvd., Ste. 200
Lanham, MD 20706
www.rowman.com
Falcon and FalconGuides are registered trademarks and Make Adventure Your Story is a trademark of The Rowman & Littlefield Publishing Group, Inc.

Distributed by NATIONAL BOOK NETWORK
Copyright © 2011 The Rowman & Littlefield Publishing Group, Inc.
This FalconGuides Edition 2019
Maps by Melissa Baker

British Library Cataloguing in Publication Information available

Library of Congress Cataloging-in-Publication Data available

ISBN 978-1-4930-3873-2 (paperback)
ISBN 978-1-4930-3874-9 (e-book)

♾™ The paper used in this publication meets the minimum requirements of American National Standard for Information Sciences—Permanence of Paper for Printed Library Materials, ANSI/NISO Z39.48-1992.

Printed in the United States of America

Contents

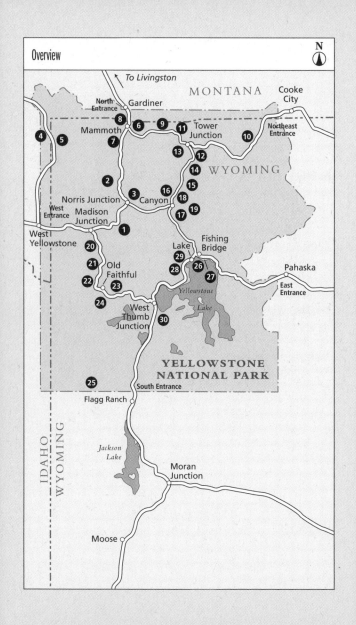

To Livingston

MONTANA

Cooke City

North Entrance

Gardiner

8

6

9

11

Tower Junction

10

Northeast Entrance

Mammoth

7

5

4

13

12

WYOMING

2

14

3

16

15

Norris Junction

Canyon

18

Madison Junction

17

19

West Entrance

1

Fishing Bridge

West Yellowstone

Lake

20

29

Pahaska

21

Old Faithful

28

26

27

East Entrance

22

23

Yellowstone Lake

24

West Thumb Junction

30

YELLOWSTONE NATIONAL PARK

25

South Entrance

Flagg Ranch

IDAHO

WYOMING

Jackson Lake

Moran Junction

Moose

Southwest Region

Southeast Region

Introduction

What Is a "Best Easy" Day Hike?

While researching and writing a much larger book on Yellowstone called *Hiking Yellowstone National Park*, I had frequent discussions with rangers on what kind of information hikers most requested. I also had the same discussions with many hikers out on the trails.

It seems, in general, that the park has two types of visitors—those who want to spend several days experiencing the depth of the Yellowstone backcountry and those who have only a day or two and would like a choice sampling of the special features of Yellowstone. This book is for the second group.

Hiking Yellowstone National Park covers almost every section of trail in the park, including those that are neither best nor easy. *Best Easy Day Hikes Yellowstone National Park* includes only shorter, less strenuous hikes that are among the nicest in the park. Most are short, but a few are longer. With a few exceptions, none have steep upgrades. All hikes are on easy-to-follow trails with no off-trail sections. It's also easy to get to the trailheads of all hikes in this book, and you can get there with any two-wheel-drive vehicle.

Some of the hikes in this book might not seem easy to some hikers but will be easy to others. To help you decide, I've ranked the hikes from easiest to hardest. I also listed the approximate hiking time required for each hike, but this means hiking time only, not time spent watching wildlife, photographing wildflowers, fishing, taking naps or the many other ways we enjoy the wilderness. Please keep in mind that short does not always equal easy. Other factors such as elevation gain and trail conditions have to be considered.

Be Prepared

Hiking in Yellowstone is generally safe. Still, hikers should be prepared, whether they are out for a short stroll or venturing into the secluded backcountry. Some specific advice:

- Know the basics of first aid, including how to treat bleeding, bites and stings, and fractures, strains, or sprains. Pack a first-aid kit on each excursion.

- Familiarize yourself with the symptoms of heat exhaustion and heat stroke. Heat exhaustion symptoms include heavy sweating, muscle cramps, headache, dizziness, and fainting. Should you or any of your hiking party exhibit any of these symptoms, cool the victim down immediately by rehydrating and getting him or her to an air-conditioned location. Cold showers also help reduce body temperature. Heat stroke is much more serious: The victim may lose consciousness and the skin is hot and dry to the touch. In this event, call 911 immediately.

- Regardless of the weather, your body needs a lot of water while hiking. A full 32-ounce bottle is the minimum for these short hikes, but more is always better. Bring a full water bottle, whether water is available along the trail or not.

- Don't drink from streams, rivers, creeks, or lakes without treating or filtering the water first. Waterways and water bodies may host a variety of contaminants, including giardia, which can cause serious intestinal unrest.

- Prepare for extremes of both heat and cold by dressing in layers.
- Yellowstone is bear country, so familiarize yourself with proper behavior (see my book *Bear Aware* for complete information). Stay alert and watch for signs of recent bear activity on the trail (piles of scat, overturned rocks and logs, etc.). Make noise while hiking to alert bears to your presence—the last thing you want to do is surprise a bear on the trail. Finally, heed all bear warnings or trail closures posted by park officials. By being smart, you can safely hike in bear country and, if you're lucky, you might even see one of the magnificent creatures (from a safe distance, of course).

Leave No Trace

Going into a national park such as Yellowstone is like visiting a famous museum. You obviously do not want to leave your mark on any art treasure in the museum. If everybody going through the museum left one little mark, the piece of art would be quickly destroyed—and of what value is a big building full of trashed art? The same goes for a famous wilderness such as Yellowstone, which is as magnificent as any masterpiece by any artist. If we all left just one little mark on the landscape, the wilderness would soon be despoiled.

A wilderness can accommodate human use as long as everybody behaves. But a few thoughtless or uninformed visitors can ruin it for everybody. All hikers have a responsibility to know and follow leave-no-trace principles. An important source of these principles can be found in the book *Leave No Trace*.

The wilderness is shrinking, and the number of users is mushrooming. More and more hiking areas show unsightly signs of heavy use.

Consequently a new code of ethics is growing out of the necessity of coping with the unending waves of people who want a perfect wilderness experience. Today we all must leave no clues that we have gone before. Canoeists can look behind the canoe and see no trace of their passing. Hikers should have the same goal. Enjoy the wilderness but leave no trace of your visit.

Here are some basic guidelines for preserving the environment in Yellowstone:

- Be prepared. Bring or wear clothes to protect you from cold, heat, or rain. Use maps to navigate (and do not rely solely on the maps included in this book).

- Avoid damaging trailside soils and plants by remaining on the established route. This is also a good rule of thumb for avoiding trailside irritants, like poison ivy.

- Pack out all your own trash, including biodegradable items like orange peels. You might also pack out garbage left by less considerate hikers. Use outhouses at trailheads or along the trail, and keep water sources clean.

- Don't pick wildflowers or gather rocks, antlers, feathers, and other treasures along the trail. Removing these items will only take away from the next hiker's experience.

- Don't approach or feed any wild creatures—the ground squirrel eyeing your snack food is best able to survive if it remains self-reliant. Control pets at all times.

- Be kind to other visitors. Yield to other trail users when appropriate.

How to Use This Guide

This guide is designed to be simple and easy to use. Each hike has a map and summary information with the trail's vital statistics including length and approximate hiking time. Directions to the trailhead (including GPS coordinates) are also provided, along with a general description of what you'll see along the hike. Key Points sets forth mileages between significant landmarks along the trail. Some hikes are self-explanatory and do not require Key Points.

Types of Hikes

The hikes in this book fall into three categories:

Loop: Starts and finishes at the same trailhead, with no (or very little) retracing of your steps.

Lollipop: Starts and finishes at the same trailhead, with a short segment that retraces your steps (the stick on the end of the loop, hence a lollipop).

Shuttle: A point-to-point trip that requires two vehicles (one left at the other end of the trail or a prearranged pickup at a designated time and place).

Out and back: Traveling to a specific destination, then retracing your steps back to the trailhead.

Ranking the Hikes

The following list ranks the hikes in this book from easiest to hardest:

9   Forces of the Northern Range Trail

6   Boiling River

Trail Finder

Best Hikes for Geysers and Thermal Activity

Best Wheelchair-Accessible Hikes

Best Hikes for Waterfalls

Best Hikes for Great Views

Best Hikes for Children

Best Hikes for Wildflowers

Best Hikes for Wildlife Watching

Best Hikes for Solitude

Best Hikes for Anglers

Best Hikes for an Easy Overnighter

Map Legend

══〔191〕══	US Highway
════	National Park Road
════	Local Road
= = = =	Unpaved Road
▬▬▬▬	Featured Trail
- - - - -	Trail
～～～	River/Creek
⬭	Lake
⤳	Marsh
⟃	Spring
≋	Waterfall
▭	National Park
⌣	Bridge
▲	Camping
▲	Mountain Peak
▬	Lodging
🅿	Parking
🌁	Picnic Area
■	Point of Interest/Structure
👫	Ranger Station
🚻	Restrooms
○	Town
❶	Trailhead
🔍	Viewpoint/Overlook
❓	Visitor/Information Center

Northwest Region

1 Artists Paintpots

Starting point: Artists Paintpots Trailhead

Distance: 1.2 miles (1.9 kilometers) out and back

Approximate hiking time: 1 hour or less

Best months: June through Sept

Maps: Trails Illustrated (Mammoth Hot Springs); Norris Junction USGS quad

Finding the trailhead: Drive for 3.7 miles south from the Norris Junction or 9.1 miles north of the Madison Junction on the Norris-Madison section of the Grand Loop Road and turn right (east) onto the short spur road to the Artist Paintpots Trailhead, which is a short drive from the main road. Trailhead GPS coordinates: N44° 41.786'/ W110° 46.476'

The Hike

This short hike skirts the south edge of massive Gibbon Meadows and stays in the unburned lodgepole all the way. The trail is partly boardwalk and the rest is double wide, flat, and easy. Since elk commonly use Gibbon Meadows, you might see some on the way to the paintpots. However, you probably won't see many people. Even though this trail goes to several interesting thermal features, it doesn't get nearly the use as the trails in the geyser basins around Old Faithful.

At the end of the hike on the slopes of Paintpot Hill, the trail makes a convenient little loop that provides good views of the major thermal features, primarily colorful paintpot formations (which early explorers thought resembled an artist's palette) as well as hot pools and steam vents. To protect both yourself and these fragile natural features, stay on the designated trail.

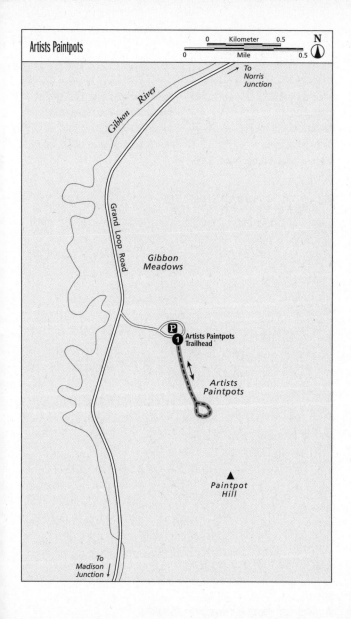

Artists Paintpots

Gibbon River

To Norris Junction

Grand Loop Road

Gibbon Meadows

P
1 Artists Paintpots Trailhead

Artists Paintpots

Paintpot Hill

To Madison Junction

0   Kilometer   0.5

0   Mile   0.5

N

2 Grizzly Lake

Starting point: Grizzly Lake Trail-head (1K8)
Distance: 3.6 miles (5.8 kilome-ters) out and back
Approximate hiking time: 2 to 2.5 hours

Best months: July through Sept
Maps: Trails Illustrated (Mammoth Hot Springs); Obsidian Cliff and Mount Holmes USGS quad

Finding the trailhead: Drive south 15.2 miles from Mammoth or 6 miles north of Norris on the Mammoth-Norris section of the Grand Loop Road and park at the trailhead, a pullout on the west side of the road. Trailhead GPS coordinates: N44° 48.786' / W110° 47.972'

The Hike

The trail starts out nice and flat as it crosses Obsidian Creek on a footbridge and goes through a large meadow just south of Beaver Lake. At the west side of the meadow, the trail starts switchbacking up the side of the ridge. Also at this point, you may see a sign for the Howard Eaton Trail going from here to Mammoth, but that trail has been abandoned by the National Park Service (NPS).

The Grizzly Lake Trail stays on top of the ridge for 0.25 mile or more before switchbacking down the other side to the north end of the lake. When you reach the 136-acre lake, the trail follows the shoreline for about 100 yards before reaching the outlet of the lake. If you're staying overnight, you have to carefully cross the outlet on a logjam to reach the campsites along Straight Creek below the lake.

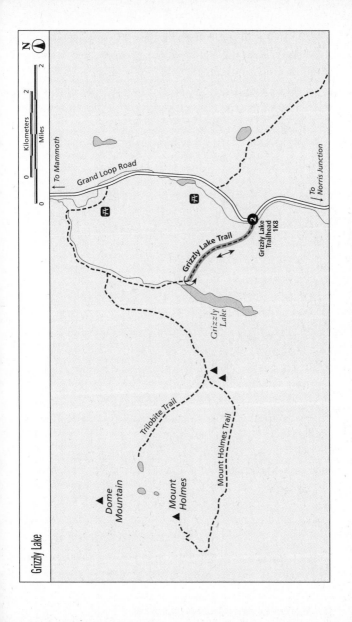

Grizzly Lake

N

Kilometers
0   2

Miles
0   2

To Mammoth ←

Grand Loop Road

To Norris Junction ↓

Grizzly Lake Trailhead
1K8

Grizzly Lake Trail

Grizzly Lake

Trilobite Trail

Mount Holmes Trail

Dome Mountain

Mount Holmes

The trail is in great shape all the way. It winds through a burned forest the entire distance except for the large meadow near the trailhead and a few small meadows on top of the ridge. Grizzly Lake is a beautiful mountain lake tucked between two forested ridges, but it has been in the path of several forest fires.

3 Ice Lake

Starting point: Ice Lake Trail-head (4K2)
Distance: 4.5 mile (7.3 kilometer) loop
Approximate hiking time: 2 to 3 hours

Best months: July through Sept
Maps: Trails Illustrated; Mammoth Hot Springs, Norris Junction and Crystal Falls USGS quads

Finding the trailhead: Drive 3.3 miles east from Norris Junction or 8.2 miles east from Canyon and park at the Ice Lake Trailhead and parking area on the north side of the road. The Little Gibbon Falls Trailhead is about 0.25 farther down the road, but not well-marked. Trailhead GPS coordinates: N44° 45.531' / W110° 39.267'

The Hike

The trail to Ice Lake gets fairly heavy traffic, but most hikers go out and back to the lake. Few hikers turn this into one of the few easy loop trips in the park, as described here. In addition to making a nice day hike, Ice Lake provides a pleasant destination for an easy overnighter.

Ice Lake is fairly large and deep, and the lodgepole forest grows tight against the lakeshore. The fires of 1988 burned much of the landscape around the lake.

The first part of the trail to Ice Lake is good enough for wheelchairs but only up to backcountry campsite 4D3. Beyond this point the trail becomes a normal backcountry single-track. It traverses the west end of the lake and joins the Howard Eaton Trail just after rounding the end of the lake.

Turn right (east) at this junction and follow the north shore of the lake, going by 4D1 shortly after the junction.

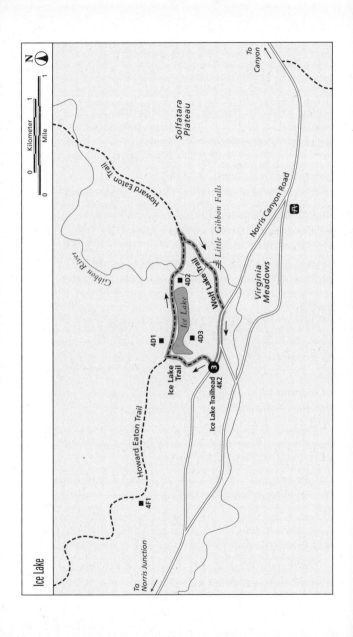

Ice Lake

N

0   1 Kilometer

0   1 Mile

Howard Eaton Trail

Gibbon River

Ice Lake

Ice Lake Trail

4D1

4D2

4D3

4F1

Wolf Lake Trail

Little Gibbon Falls

Solfatara Plateau

Ice Lake Trailhead
4K2

3

Howard Eaton Trail

To Norris Junction

To Canyon

Norris Canyon Road

Virginia Meadows

You pass the spur trail to 4D2 at the east end of the lake and ford the Gibbon River shortly thereafter. In summer this river could be described as a creek, and you'll have no problem fording it. After the ford the trail continues east for another 0.7 mile to the junction with the Little Gibbon Falls Trail (called Wolf Lake Trail on some maps).

Turn right (south) at this junction and go another mile or so to 25-foot Little Gibbon Falls, which actually resembles the larger Gibbon Falls downstream along the Norris-Madison section of the Grand Loop Road. From the falls the trail drops into spacious Virginia Meadows along the Gibbon River until you reach the highway.

The trail is in good shape and stays in a mostly burned lodgepole forest much of the way, including all around the lake. The trail gets a little rougher on the last leg of the trip by Little Gibbon Falls, but it's still distinct with the exception of one spot near the highway where it disappears for about 100 yards in the lush meadow along the river. An orange marker on the other side of the meadow marks the route.

When you reach the highway, you have to walk about 0.5-mile along the paved road back to your vehicle.

Options: Hikers can hike out and back to Ice Lake or Little Gibbon Falls.

Key Points

0.0	Ice Lake Trailhead.
0.3 (0.5)	Spur trail to backcountry campsite 4D3.
0.5 (0.8)	Ice Lake.
0.6 (1.0)	Junction with Howard Eaton Trail; turn right.
0.8 (1.3)	Backcountry campsite 4D1.

1.5 (2.4) Backcountry campsite 4D2.

2.3 (3.7) Junction with Little Gibbon Falls/Wolf Lake Trail; turn right.

3.4 (5.5) Little Gibbon Falls.

4.0 (6.5) Norris-Canyon Road; turn right.

4.5 (7.3) Ice Lake Trailhead.

4 Bacon Rind Creek

Starting point: Bacon Rind Trailhead (WK4)
Distance: 4.2 miles (6.5 kilometers) out and back
Approximate hiking time: 2 to 2.5 hours

Best months: July through Sept
Maps: Trails Illustrated (Mammoth Hot Springs); Divide Lake USGS quad

Finding the trailhead: Drive south from Belgrade or north from West Yellowstone on US 191 to 14.2 miles north of the US 191/US 89 junction, turn west on the Bacon Rind Road between mileposts 22 and 23, and follow the gravel road 0.3 mile to the trailhead. Trailhead GPS coordinates: N44° 57.319' / W111° 04.245'

The Hike

This trail has the distinction of being the only trail heading west from the Gallatin Valley in the park. After the park boundary (at the 2.1-mile mark), the trail keeps going up into the Lee Metcalf Wilderness in the Gallatin National Forest. However, the trail gets faint after the park boundary. The map may show the trail crossing Bacon Rind Creek before the park boundary, but it stays on the north side of the stream.

This is a flat, easy trail along the bottomlands of Bacon Rind Creek. The stream contains a small population of rainbow trout, and willow thickets along the creek provide hiding places for moose and grizzly bears. If you plan to fish (catch-and-release only), be sure to get a park fishing permit.

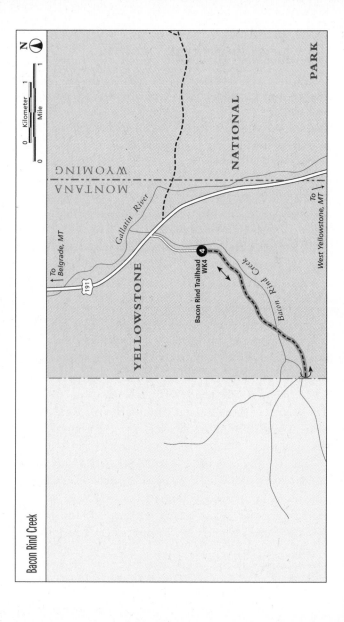

Bacon Rind Creek

The trail follows the meandering stream as it winds its way through a beautiful mountain meadow with a strange (almost man-made-like) square-shaped hill in the middle of it. When you reach the park boundary, which is well signed, take a break before returning to the trailhead.

5 Fan Creek

Starting point: Fawn Pass Trailhead (WK5)
Distance: 6.0 to 12.2 miles (9.8 to 19.6 kilometers) out and back
Difficulty: Moderate

Best months: July through Oct
Maps: Trails Illustrated (Mammoth Hot Springs); Divide Lake and Quadrant Mountain USGS quads

Finding the trailhead: Drive south from Belgrade or north from West Yellowstone on US 191 to just south of milepost 22 and park in the Fawn Pass Trailhead on the east side of the road, 13.5 miles north of the US 191/US 89 junction. Trailhead GPS coordinates: N44° 57' 2.422" / W111° 3' 32.335"

The Hike

After hiking this trail, you could be easily convinced that Fan Creek is a shortened version of the original name Fantastic Creek. This is definitely one of the most beautiful mountain valleys in the park.

In addition to its growing popularity with hikers, Fan Creek gets moderate to heavy use from trail riders taking long loop trips over to Gardner's Hole and back over Fawn Pass.

The terrain doesn't completely open up until after the Fawn Pass Trail junction, where you turn left (northeast). You can go as far as 6.1 miles, where the East Fork and the North Fork merge, or you can go any shorter distance. At about 1.8 miles, note the spur trail to WC2. This was formerly the main trail, but the NPS has rerouted this section

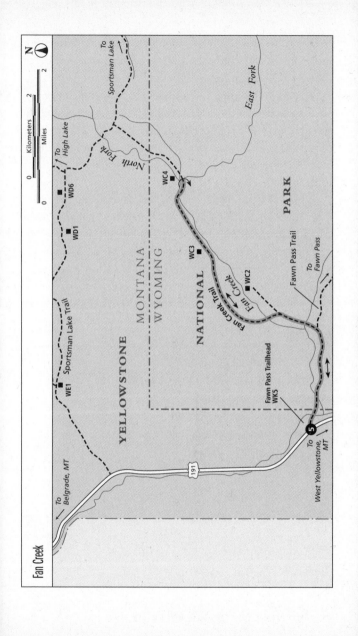

Fan Creek

N

To Belgrade, MT

To Sportsman Lake

To High Lake

North Fork

Sportsman Lake Trail

WE1

WD6

WD1

WC4

WC3

WC2

Fall Creek Trail

Fan Creek Trail

East Fork

YELLOWSTONE

MONTANA
WYOMING

NATIONAL   PARK

Fawn Pass Trail

To Fawn Pass

Fawn Pass Trailhead
WK5

5

191

West Yellowstone, MT

Kilometers   2

Miles   2

of trail to the north side of Fan Creek. At about 2 miles you ford Fan Creek, which also makes a good turnaround. The crossing is less than knee-deep and easy after mid-July.

If you're looking for a moderate day hike, possibly combined with some stream fishing, Fan Creek would be an excellent choice. There are no big hills, and the trail is in terrific shape the entire way. You might want to go early or stay late to watch elk and moose, which are quite abundant in the area.

The area east of upper Fan Creek (after campsite WC4) is a part of the Gallatin Bear Management Area and closed to off-trail travel from May 1 to November 10.

Because of wet trail conditions, the NPS prohibits the use of stock on this route until conditions allow it, which is no earlier than July 1. So during June and sometimes early July, it's hikers only.

Key Points

0.0	Fawn Pass Trailhead.
1.3 (2.1)	Fawn Pass Trail junction; turn left.
1.8 (2.4)	Spur trail to WC2.
2.0 (2.7)	Fan Creek Ford.
6.1 (9.8)	Confluence of North and East Forks of Fan Creek.
12.2 (19.6)	Fawn Pass Trailhead.

6 Boiling River

Starting point: Boiling River Trailhead

Distance: 1.0 mile (1.6 kilometers) out and back

Approximate hiking time: 1 hour or less

Best months: Mid-May through mid-Oct

Maps: Trails Illustrated (Mammoth Hot Springs); Gardiner USGS quad

Finding the trailhead: Drive south of Gardiner on the North Entrance Road through the entrance station for 2.5 miles and turn either right or left into one of the Boiling River parking lots. There is so much traffic on this trail that the National Park Service (NPS) has expanded the parking lot to the west side of the road. The trailhead is in the northeast corner of the parking lot on the east side of the road. Trailhead GPS coordinates: N44° 59.067' / W110° 41.478'

The Hike

Until the mid–1980s, the Boiling River was mostly a social hot tub for locals and park employees. Since then the NPS has made it an official trail and swimming hole.

The Boiling River is created by a massive hot spring discharge 2 feet deep and 6 feet wide (probably from the Mammoth Hot Springs) flowing into the Gardner River.

The river has never been known to "boil," but it does get comfortably warm, and people have been soaking in this hot water for decades. Early promoters touted it as the only place you could catch a trout and boil it on the hook.

Now the NPS has constructed a nice trail along the banks of the Gardner River to the hot spring, and it has become a very popular, short day hike. On a hot summer

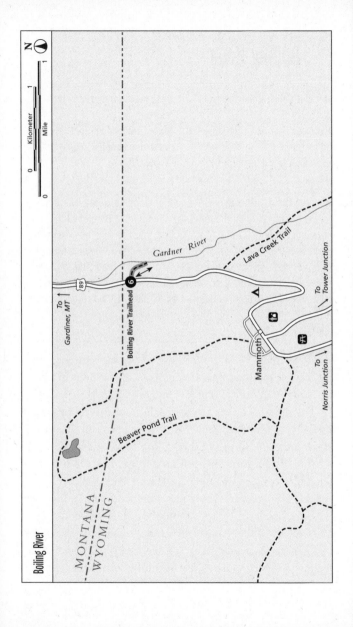

Boiling River

N

0   Kilometer   1

0   Mile   1

Gardner River

89

To
Gardiner, MT

6 Boiling River Trailhead

Lava Creek Trail

To
Tower Junction

Mammoth

To
Norris Junction

Beaver Pond Trail

MONTANA
WYOMING

afternoon, expect to see dozens of people at the hot spring. The trail is easy and flat all the way.

Because of the extreme popularity of this hike (more than 200 hikers per day), the NPS has established special regulations. The trail is open only from 5:00 a.m. to 9:00 p.m. (even shorter hours during winter), and pets, bicycles, soap, food or beverages, and public nudity are prohibited. You can only swim in the Gardner River, not in the hot spring where it emerges from under a travertine ledge.

Another unusual tidbit of information is that this trail is on the Forty-fifth Parallel, precisely halfway between the North Pole and the South Pole.

Options: You can also hike down to the Boiling River from the Mammoth Campground on an unofficial trail (not on park map), but this is a much tougher hike involving a 300-foot hill to get back to the campground.

7 Bunsen Peak

Starting point: Bunsen Peak Trailhead (1K4)
Distance: 4.2 miles (6.8 kilometers) out and back
Approximate hiking time: 2.5 to 3 hours

Best months: Mid-July through Sept
Maps: Trails Illustrated (Mammoth Hot Springs); Mammoth USGS quad

Finding the trailhead: Drive 4.8 miles south of Mammoth on the Mammoth-Norris section of the Grand Loop Road to just past the Golden Gate Bridge and park on the left (east) in the Glen Creek Trailhead parking lot. Trailhead GPS coordinates: N44° 46.004' / W110° 43.872'

The Hike

This trail offers the easiest way to get a spectacular mountaintop view of the northwestern corner of the park. However, some people wouldn't call this an easy hike. You go up 1,300 feet in 2.1 miles. Fortunately the trail is superbly switchbacked to minimize the impact of the elevation gain. In addition, the scenery along the way tends to absorb you, so you don't focus on the effort it takes to reach the summit. If you want to be able to say you climbed a mountain in Yellowstone Park, this hike (or Mount Washburn) would be your least strenuous way to meet that goal.

Be sure to bring water, though. You won't find any on the mountain unless you hike in June or early July, when you can find snowbanks.

From the top you can see the large meadow below to the west known as Gardner's Hole and, of course, a river

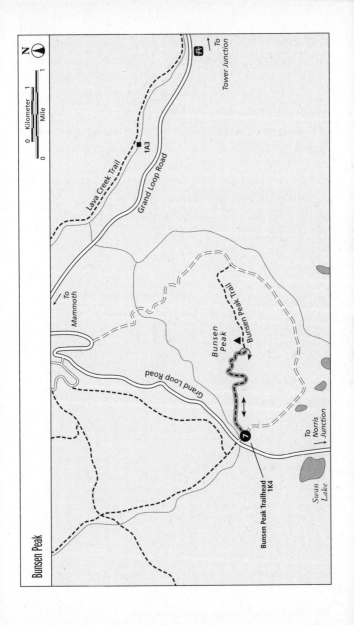

Bunsen Peak

N

0   Kilometer   1

0   Mile   1

Lava Creek Trail

1A3

Grand Loop Road

To Tower Junction

To Mammoth

Grand Loop Road

Bunsen Peak

Bunsen Peak Trail

Bunsen Peak Trailhead
1K4

To Norris Junction

Swan Lake

runs through it (the Gardner River). You can also see the town of Gardiner over the top of Terrace Mountain, along with Mammoth Terrace in the foreground—and awesome 10,992-foot Electric Peak to the west, 10,336-foot Mount Holmes to the south, the mighty Absarokas to the north, and just about everything else. The telecommunications equipment on the summit is somewhat distracting, but the view is undeniably overwhelming.

You might want to hike this early in the morning before the afternoon heat makes the climb harder. If you go early, bring along some binoculars so you can watch wildlife from the summit.

8 Beaver Ponds

Starting point: Sepulcher Mountain Trailhead (1K1) in Mammoth

Distance: 5.1 mile (8.2 kilometer) loop

Approximate hiking time: 3 to 4 hours

Best months: May through Sept

Maps: Trails Illustrated (Mammoth Hot Springs); Mammoth USGS quad

Finding the trailhead: Drive south from Gardiner to Mammoth Hot Springs. The trailhead is on the right (west) just below the main hot springs by Liberty Cap on the north edge of the thermal area. Park in the large lot across the road from the trailhead. Trailhead GPS coordinates: N44° 58.714' / W110° 41.521'

The Hike

If you stay at Mammoth and have some extra time to get away from the traffic-choked roads, this gentle 5.1-mile loop trail is a great option. There is an excellent chance of seeing elk (if you haven't already seen enough right in Mammoth), moose, and black bear.

The trail begins just to the right (north) of Clematis Creek before Liberty Cap. After about a hundred yards, it crosses Clematis Creek on a bridge and starts gradually climbing uphill with brilliant colors of Mammoth Hot Springs on the left (south).

At 0.2 mile you reach the junction with the Golden Gate/Howard Eaton Trail, which takes you behind the hot springs and to Terrace Mountain. Turn right (west) and continue toward Beaver Ponds. The trail crosses another bridge and climbs more steeply, passing one unmarked

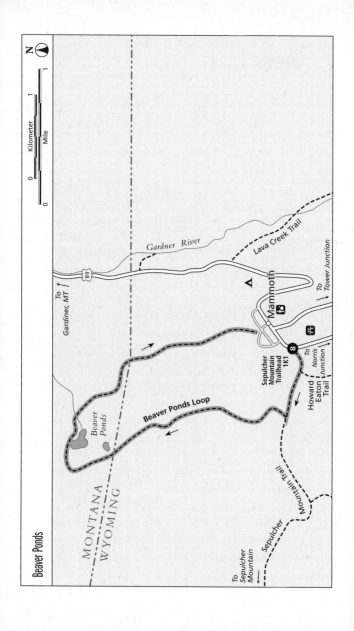

Beaver Ponds

N

Kilometer

Mile

Gardner River

Lava Creek Trail

To
Gardiner, MT

89

Mammoth

To Tower Junction

Sepulcher Mountain Trailhead 1K1

To Norris Junction

8

Howard Eaton Trail

Beaver Ponds Loop

Beaver Ponds

MONTANA
WYOMING

To Sepulcher Mountain

Sepulcher Mountain Trail

junction with an unofficial trail. Stay left and keep switch-backing uphill.

At 0.7 mile turn right (north) at the junction with the Sepulcher Mountain Trail. The junction has a unique marker. An old carved stump signals mountain trail/ranger nature trail. That old nature trail is now called the Beaver Ponds Trail.

After this junction the trail levels out and crosses meadows of dandelions and aspen. In the spring you might see some larkspur and shooting stars along the way. This section of trail offers sweeping views of Gardner River Valley and across to the Absaroka Range to the north.

After a short descent the trail passes the first of several ponds. The Beaver Ponds consist of several marshy lakes graced by cattails and a few lily pads.

The return trip is relatively flat across a sagebrush plateau with good scenery all around, especially Mount Everts (which would be better described as a ridge) across Gardner Canyon. When you see the town of Mammoth, the trail intersects an old road. Again, stay right. This last 0.1-mile descent to Mammoth terminates in the parking lot behind the main lodge, a short walk back to the trailhead.

Key Points

0.0	Sepulcher Mountain Trailhead.
0.2 (0.3)	Junction with Howard Eaton Trail; turn right.
0.7 (1.1)	Junction with Sepulcher Mountain Trail; turn right.
3.0 (4.8)	Beaver Ponds; turn right.
5.0 (8.1)	Intersection with old road.
5.1 (8.2)	Mammoth Hotel parking lot.

Northeast Region

⑨ Forces of the Northern Range Trail

Starting point: Forces of the Northern Range Trail Trailhead
Distance: 0.7 mile (1.1 kilometer) loop
Approximate hiking time: 1 hour or less

Best months: May through Sept
Maps: Trails Illustrated (Mammoth Hot Springs); Blacktail Deer Creek USGS quad

Finding the trailhead: Drive 8.2 miles east from Mammoth Hot Springs or 9.8 miles west from Tower Junction and pull into a turnout on the south side of the road. Trailhead GPS coordinates: N44° 57.570' / W110° 33.488'

The Hike

Originally constructed to provide interpretation in the aftermath of the historic fires of 1988 and called the Children's Fire Trail, the National Park Service (NPS) has now expanded the scope of the interpretation to include other forces of nature, not just forest fires. And now, it's for adult children, too.

The wheelchair-accessible trail is entirely on a boardwalk, with multiple interpretive displays telling the story of how forest fires, volcanoes, and glaciers shaped the landscape of Yellowstone and help in identifying local plants and animals. It's a "lollipop" loop, complete with benches for resting and with several out-and-back spur trails to interpretive displays.

10 Trout Lake

Starting point: Trout Lake Trailhead

Distance: 1.2 miles (1.9 kilometers) out and back

Approximate hiking time: 1 to 2 hours

Best months: June through Sept

Maps: Trails Illustrated (Tower/Canyon); Mount Hornaday USGS quad

Finding the trailhead: Drive 17 miles east of Tower Junction or 11.4 miles west of the Northeast Entrance and park in the turnout on the north side of the road, 1.8 miles west of Pebble Creek Campground. Trailhead GPS coordinates: N44° 54.202' / W110° 07.044'

The Hike

This trail, which is not shown on some park maps, is popular with anglers in the Lamar Valley, but it also provides a pleasant day hike for non-anglers. The rainbow-cutthroat hybrids in the lake are big and hard to catch but incredibly rewarding for the successful angler.

From the trailhead the trail goes steeply uphill. The path climbs under Douglas-fir cover to the inlet of the lake, which rests in a big meadow filled with wildflowers. The trail around the lake provides more hiking.

The 12-acre lake is catch-and-release fishing (don't forget to get a park fishing permit). But the inlet is closed to fishing to protect spawning trout, which provide quite the show for onlookers. But be careful not to disturb the spawners during their crucial time.

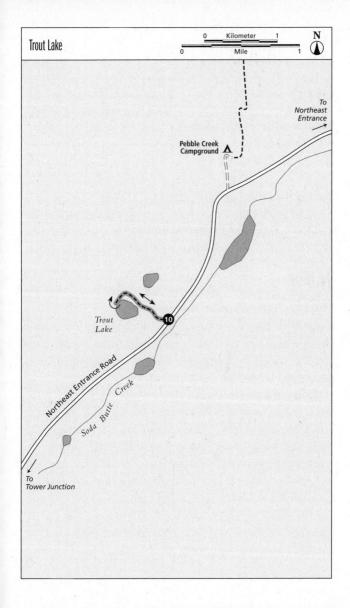

Trout Lake

0 Kilometer 1
0 Mile 1

N

To
Northeast
Entrance

Pebble Creek
Campground

Trout
Lake

10

Northeast Entrance Road

Soda Butte Creek

To
Tower Junction

11 Hellroaring Creek

Starting point: Hellroaring Trailhead (2K8)
Distance: 4.0 miles (6.5 kilometers) out and back
Approximate hiking time: 2 to 3 hours

Best months: May through Sept
Maps: Trails Illustrated (Tower/Canyon); Tower Junction USGS quad

Finding the trailhead: Drive 14.3 miles east from Mammoth or 3.7 miles west from Tower and pull into the Hellroaring Trailhead. The actual trailhead is 0.3 mile down an unpaved service road. Trailhead GPS coordinates: N44° 56.933' / W110° 27.046'

The Hike

This is the first section of the longer hikes through the Black Canyon of the Yellowstone and around the Hellroaring Creek and Coyote Creek Loop. In addition to making a nice day hike, this is a great choice for the beginning backpacker, who has the choice of six excellent campsites on Hellroaring Creek.

The trail switchbacks through open timber and sagebrush meadows for the first mile to the suspension bridge over the Yellowstone River. This isn't the suspension bridge you saw in the Indiana Jones movies. It's steel and sturdy. From the bridge, the trail goes into the open landscape in the Yellowstone and Hellroaring Valleys.

The trail is in superb condition all the way. You pass by two trail junctions, the first to Tower and the second up Coyote Creek. Go left (west) at both junctions.

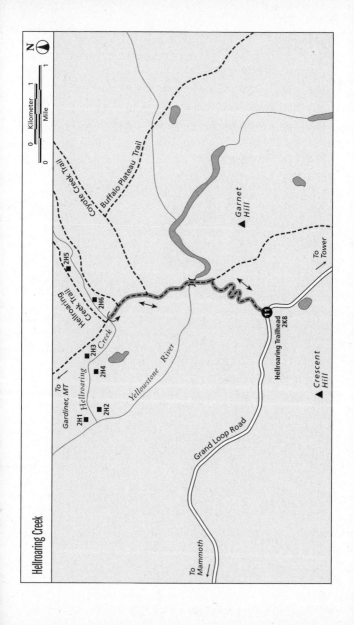

Hellroaring Creek

N

0   Kilometer   1

0   Mile   1

Coyote Creek Trail

Buffalo Plateau Trail

Hellroaring Creek Trail

2H5

2H6

2H3

2H4

2H2

2H1

To Gardiner, MT

Hellroaring Creek

Yellowstone River

Garnet Hill

Hellroaring Trailhead 2K8

To Tower

Crescent Hill

Grand Loop Road

To Mammoth

Key Points

0.0   Hellroaring Trailhead.

0.8 (1.3)   Junction with trail to Tower; turn left.

1.0 (1.6)   Suspension bridge.

1.6 (2.6)   Junction with trail to Coyote Creek and Buffalo Plateau; turn left.

2.0 (3.2)   Hellroaring Creek.

4.0 (6.5)   Hellroaring Trailhead.

12 Yellowstone River Picnic Area Trail

Starting point: Yellowstone River Picnic Area Trailhead (2K7)
Distance: 4.0 miles (6.5 kilometers) out and back
Approximate hiking time: 2 to 3 hours

Best months: May through Sept
Maps: Trails Illustrated (Tower/Canyon); Tower Junction USGS quad

Finding the trailhead: Drive 1.3 miles east of Tower Junction and pull into the Yellowstone River Picnic Area on the south side of the road. Trailhead GPS coordinates: N44° 55.023' / W110° 24.005'

The Hike

This is a delightful day hike when you need some exercise after a picnic. You can go as far as 2 miles before the trail joins the Specimen Ridge Trail, or you can walk along the ridge overlooking the Yellowstone for whatever distance suits you before returning to the picnic area.

Several unofficial trails leave the picnic area, and they join up with the official trail about 0.5 mile later. The official trail starts by the trail sign on the east side of the picnic area and appears to head east, but it quickly turns south and gradually climbs up to the ridge above the river.

After a short climb the trail levels out and goes along the rim of the Yellowstone—great scenery, but if you have children, watch them carefully. It would be a serious fall down into the river bottom.

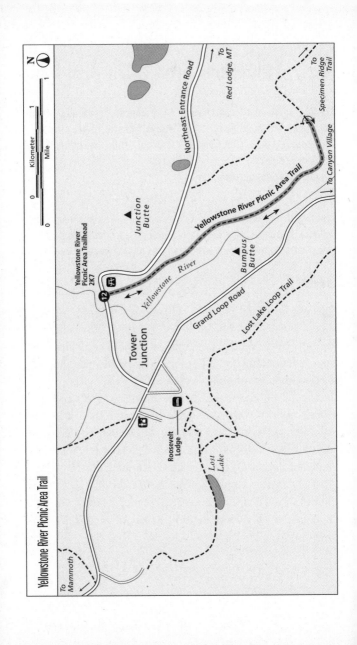

Yellowstone River Picnic Area Trail

N

0   1   Kilometer

0   1   Mile

To Red Lodge, MT

Northeast Entrance Road

To Specimen Ridge Trail

Yellowstone River Picnic Area Trail

To Canyon Village

Junction Butte

Yellowstone River

Yellowstone River Picnic Area Trailhead 2K7

Bumpus Butte

Grand Loop Road

Tower Junction

Lost Lake Loop Trail

Roosevelt Lodge

Lost Lake

To Mammoth

13 Lost Lake

Starting point: Roosevelt Lodge
Distance: 2.5 mile (4.0 kilometer) loop. Out and back or shuttle also available
Approximate hiking time: 2 to 3 hours

Best months: June through Sept
Maps: Trails Illustrated (Tower/Canyon); Tower Junction USGS quad

Finding the trailhead: From Tower Junction, drive south and park at Roosevelt Lodge. The trail starts at the south edge of the lodge. It's a little confusing right at the south side of the lodge where the trail starts. Take the trail to Lost Lake, not the trail to Lost Creek Falls. Trailhead GPS coordinates: N44° 54.757' / W110° 24.986'

The Hike

Lost Lake is a charming little mountain lake (only six acres) lost in the forest behind Roosevelt Lodge. The trail is distinct and in great shape the entire way.

Behind the lodge, the trail crosses a bridge and then forks. Go left (southwest) and start climbing—mostly gradual with a few steep pitches at first—through unburned forest on switchbacks about 200 feet up to the top of the ridge. You might see a junction with an unofficial trail about halfway up the hill; if so, go right to stay on the official trail. On top of the ridge, you reach an official junction. The left trail goes east to Lost Creek Falls and Tower Fall Campground. Go right (west) for 0.2 mile to Lost Lake, which is preceded by a big meadow. The lake is shallow with yellow pond lilies along the shoreline. Sorry, no fish.

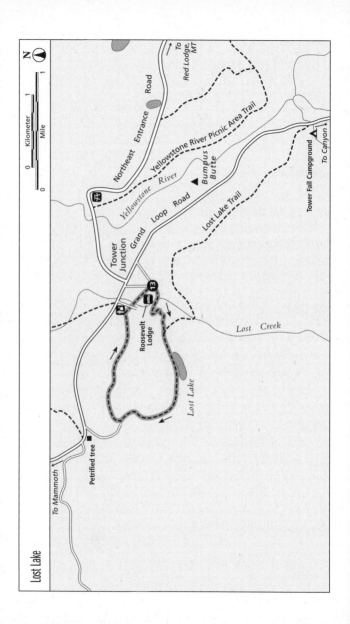

Lost Lake

From the lake keep going east until you come out in the parking lot for the Petrified Tree. You can drive here, but by walking down from the lake you can avoid retracing your steps and make a small loop out of this hike. When we hiked this trail, there was no sign marking the cutoff trail that follows the Mammoth-Tower Road back to Roosevelt Lodge, but this well-defined, heavily used trail starts at the south end of the parking lot where you come in from Lost Lake. It's marked with an orange marker. In fact, the entire trail is lined with orange markers to tell you you're on the official trail, not one of the many social trails in the area.

The trail from the Petrified Tree back to Roosevelt Lodge climbs back up to the top of the ridge and then down to behind Tower Ranger Station and comes out at the junction at the bridge behind Roosevelt Lodge to complete the loop.

Options: If you want to make this a shorter hike, walk out and back to the lake. If you want a shuttle (and a good view of Lost Creek Falls), take a left at the top of the ridge and hike another 3 miles to Tower Fall Campground. The trail comes out on the paved road up to the campground. You can walk down the road about a 0.25-mile to the general store. This is a nice, flat trail through open forest and large meadows until it drops steeply down to the campground. You can also have somebody meet you or leave a vehicle at the petrified tree parking lot to cut 0.8 (and a short climb) off the hike.

Key Points

0.0	Roosevelt Lodge.
0.1 (0.2)	Bridge and trail junction, turn left.

0.6 (0.9) Junction with Tower Falls Trail, turn right.

0.8 (1.1) Lost Lake.

1.7 (2.7) Petrified Tree parking lot.

2.3 (3.7) Tower Ranger Station.

2.4 (3.9) Bridge and trail junction, turn left.

2.5 (4.0) Roosevelt Lodge.

14 Tower Fall

Starting point: Tower Fall store	**Best months:** July through Sept
Distance: 1.0 mile (1.6 kilometers) out and back	**Maps:** Trails Illustrated (Tower/Canyon); Tower Junction USGS quad
Approximate hiking time: 1 hour or less	

Finding the trailhead: Drive 2.5 miles south of Tower Junction or 15.5 miles north of Canyon Junction on the Tower-Canyon section of the Grand Loop Road and park in the large parking lot for the Tower Fall store. Trailhead GPS coordinates: N44° 53.529' / W110° 23.222'

The Hike

The trip to Tower Fall is one of the shortest but most rewarding hikes in the park. From the overlook (about 100 yards from the store), you get a great perspective of the 132-foot waterfall. Then by walking down a double-wide, carefully switchbacked trail for another 0.5 mile, you get the rest of the story.

The trail takes you down to where Tower Creek disappears into the mighty Yellowstone River. From here, you used to be able to take a short spur trail to your left over to the foot of the falls; however, the National Park Service (NPS) has recently closed that trail because of erosion but plans to reopen it after reconstruction. If it's open when you make the trip, take it for an awesome perspective of Tower Fall.

Take along a sweater. Even on a warm August afternoon, the mist thrown up by the falls can cast a cool atmosphere

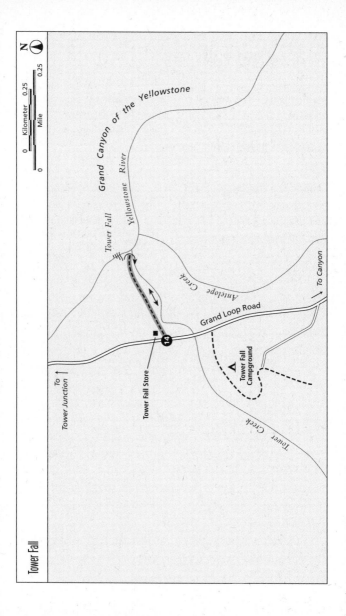

Tower Fall

over the shaded canyon gouged out by the crashing water. The 1870 Washburn party named the waterfall for the large tower-like rocks at the brink of the falls, one of which crashed to the depths of the canyon in 1986. No, luckily, there weren't any park visitors under the falls at the time!

15 Mount Washburn

Starting point: Chittenden Road Trailhead (2K6)

Distance: 5.2 miles (8.4 kilometers) out and back

Approximate hiking time: 3 to 4 hours

Best months: July through Sept

Maps: Trails Illustrated (Tower/Canyon); Mount Washburn USGS quad

Finding the trailhead: Drive 10.4 miles north of Canyon or 8.6 miles south of Tower Junction on the Tower-Canyon section of the Grand Loop Road and turn onto the well-marked Chittenden Road. Follow the gravel road for about a mile to a locked gate and a large parking lot off to the left. Trailhead GPS coordinates: N44° 50.418' / W110° 26.345'

The Hike

The Chittenden Road continues up to the top of the mountain, but it's for official use only. You have to walk or ride a mountain bike to the summit. This is a little stretch on the "easy" part (2.6 miles uphill most of the way), but undoubtedly one of the "best" hikes in the park, so it made the list.

It's nearly 1,500 feet to the top of what is left of an ancient volcano that exploded 600,000 years ago and created the Yellowstone Caldera. However, the slope of the gravel road (made for vehicles, of course) makes for easy walking. Very few vehicles use the road, so it seems like a big, wide trail.

You hike in the open slopes of Mount Washburn the entire way. If you don't see bighorn sheep on the way

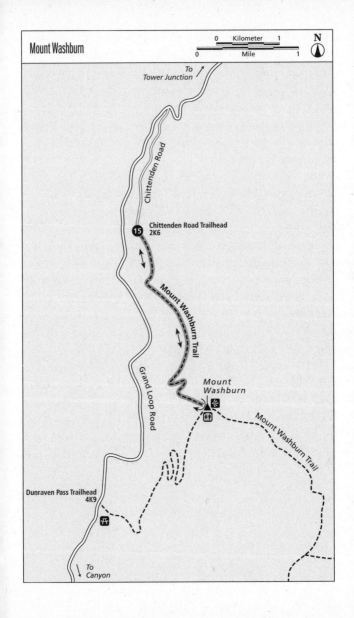

Mount Washburn

To
Tower Junction

Chittenden Road

15 Chittenden Road Trailhead
2K6

Mount Washburn Trail

Grand Loop Road

*Mount
Washburn*

Mount Washburn Trail

Dunraven Pass Trailhead
4K9

To
Canyon

up, you almost assuredly will see them on the summit, where a small herd resides most of the summer. (Please don't feed them!) Also expect to be hiking through a virtual wildflower bouquet the entire way. Mount Washburn yearly hosts an incredible abundance and diversity of alpine wildflowers. After hiking all of Yellowstone, I did not find another place that matched the wildflower showcase found on Mount Washburn.

At the summit you might be surprised to find a major structure conservatively referred to as a lookout. It has an interpretive center, 20-power telescopes for wildlife viewing, a drinking fountain, and bathrooms.

Watch the weather. You don't want to get caught on this mountain in a thunderstorm.

Options: You can also come up to the summit of Mount Washburn from Dunraven Pass, which is about the same distance and intensity as the Chittenden Road route but slightly harder on the nerves as it goes along a knife-edge ridge just before the summit.

Side trips: If you have some extra time on top, you can walk along the ridge toward Dunraven Pass for about 0.5 mile without losing much elevation. You can also hike the first part of the spur trail to Canyon, which heads off to the east through a major wildflower garden. If you want to identify every flower along the way, you'll need several hours.

16 Cascade Lake

Starting point: Cascade Lake Trail Picnic Area (4K5)

Distance: 5.0 miles (8.1 kilometers) out and back

Approximate hiking time: 2.5 to 4 hours

Best months: July through Sept

Maps: Trails Illustrated (Tower/ Canyon); Mammoth Hot Springs, Crystal Falls, Cook Peak, Canyon Village, and Mount Washburn USGS quads

Finding the trailhead: Drive 1.2 miles north of Canyon Junction and park in the trailhead parking area on the west side of the road, just south of the Cascade Lake picnic area. Trailhead GPS coordinates: N44° 45.103' / W110° 29.212'

The Hike

This is not only a great day hike but also a good choice for the beginning backpacker looking for one of his or her first nights in the wilderness. You can have lunch at the picnic area just north of the trailhead before starting to hike. You can start the hike at the trailhead or from the picnic area.

It's a short 2.5 miles to the large, deep lake, and the trail is in excellent condition the entire way and even double-wide near the picnic area. It's a flat hike through scattered forest and meadows until you get close to the lake and enter a huge meadow. In June and July the meadows along the way are ablaze with wildflowers—and full of bison, too, so be careful.

The thirty-six-acre lake has a healthy population of cutthroat and grayling, so expect to see a few anglers flaying the lake with fly rods.

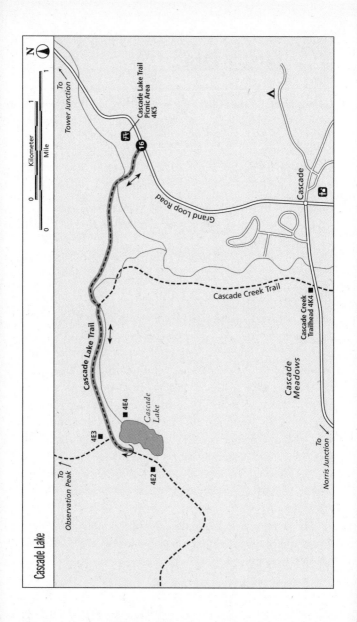

Cascade Lake

N

To
Tower Junction

Cascade Lake Trail
Picnic Area
4K5

16

Grand Loop Road

Cascade Creek Trail

Cascade
Creek
Trailhead 4K4

Cascade

Cascade Lake Trail

4E3

4E4

Cascade
Lake

4E2

To
Observation Peak

Cascade Meadows

To
Norris Junction

Kilometer

Mile

Mosquitoes like this part of the park, so to avoid these flocks of bloodsuckers, wait until August or September to hike into Cascade Lake.

Options: You can also get to Cascade Lake from the Cascade Creek Trailhead (4K4), just east of Canyon on the Canyon-Norris Cutoff Road.

Side trips: If you have time you can hike from the lake 3 miles up to the summit of Observation Peak. You can also take the 2.5-mile hike over to Grebe Lake.

Key Points

0.0	Cascade Lake Trailhead.
2.0 (3.2)	Junction with Cascade Creek Trail; turn right.
2.3 (3.7)	Spur trail to backcountry campsite 4E4.
2.4 (3.9)	Junction with trail to Observation Peak and backcountry campsite 4E3; turn left.
2.5 (4.0)	Cascade Lake.
5.0 (8.1)	Cascade Lake Trailhead.

17 Canyon Rim South

Starting point: Wapiti Lake Trailhead (4K7)

Distance: 3.5 mile (5.6 kilometer) shuttle

Approximate hiking time: 2 to 3 hours

Best months: June through Sept

Maps: The Yellowstone Association's map/brochure for Canyon; Trails Illustrated (Tower/Canyon); Canyon Village USGS quad

Finding the trailhead: Drive south 2.3 miles from the Canyon Junction, turn left (east), crossing the Chittenden Bridge, and park in the large parking area on your right immediately after crossing the bridge. Trailhead GPS coordinates: N44° 42.475' / W110° 30.036'

The Hike

There are two ways to see the sights of the South Rim of the Grand Canyon of the Yellowstone. You can drive from parking lot to parking lot, get in and out of your car several times, and call it a day. Or you can take a wonderful hike along the canyon rim to see it all and get some exercise, too.

The trail from Chittenden Bridge to Point Sublime is 3.5 miles. You can take all of it or whatever section that suits you. The scenery is world renowned the entire way with many views of the mighty Yellowstone River and its Grand Canyon, Lower Falls and Upper Falls, all the way to Point Sublime, and a view of Silver Cord Cascades plunging down into the canyon from Ribbon Lake.

The trail gets heavy use, and parts of it are paved to accommodate this popularity. Even the unpaved sections are in superb condition. Unless you go down the Uncle Tom's Trail, there aren't any steep sections, although you

Canyon Rim South

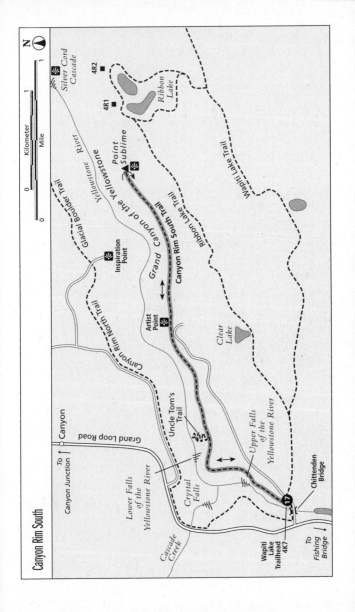

face a few short upgrades to get through small valleys and a gradual upgrade to get from the river-level trailhead to Artist Point Overlook, about 150 feet above the river.

From the trailhead the trail drops down to river level right above Upper Falls, where you get a good view of the footbridge on the other side of the river. Just before Uncle Tom's Trail parking area, you get the ideal view of Upper Falls from the Upper Falls Overlook. At Artist Point you get the picturesque view of Lower Falls and the Grand Canyon. If you stop at Artist Point, you'll miss one of the great views in the park, Point Sublime. The grand expansiveness of the canyon is spread before you at Point Sublime.

If you can't arrange to leave a vehicle, retrace your steps to the Wapiti Lake Trailhead.

Options: You can hike sections of this trail out and back or you can leave a vehicle at Artist Point to keep from retracing your steps over part of the trip. You can also combine the South Rim and North Rim hikes by leaving a vehicle at Inspiration Point and starting at Artist Point or vice versa.

Side trips: Uncle Tom's Trail is a must-see side trip. This may be the most unusual hike in the park. It's not really a trail. Instead it's a series of stairs made of steel grates, concrete, and asphalt, 328 steps from top to bottom. The "grand staircase" takes you down 500 feet in elevation to an incredible viewpoint near the base of the Lower Falls.

Although short (1 mile round-trip), this trail can be quite strenuous coming up and is not recommended for anybody with heart or lung problems. However, the National Park Service (NPS) has made it as easy as possible, with handrails much of the way and benches to rest on while climbing out of the canyon.

18 Canyon Rim North

Starting point: Wapiti Lake Trail-head (4K7)
Distance: 3.0 mile (4.8 kilometer) shuttle
Approximate hiking time: 2 to 3 hours

Best months: June through Sept
Maps: The Yellowstone Association's map/brochure for Canyon; Trails Illustrated (Tower/Canyon); Canyon Village USGS quad

Finding the trailhead: Drive south 2.3 miles from the Canyon Junction, turn left (east), crossing the Chittenden Bridge, and park in the large parking area on your right immediately after crossing the bridge. Trailhead GPS coordinates: N44° 43.297' / W110° 29.155'

The Hike

Like the South Rim, the North Rim is loaded with world-famous scenery and short side trips. It's a nice half-day hike if you take in all the sights.

From the bridge, hike to the short (about 0.25 mile) side trip to the Brink of the Upper Falls, an awe-inspiring (if not scary) view of the river plunging over the 109-foot Upper Falls.

Next along the way is Crystal Falls on Cascade Creek, a nice contrast to the Upper and Lower Falls. The trail goes over the top of the delicate waterfall. Then you reach perhaps the most memorable spot on the trip—the side trip down to the Brink of the Lower Falls, where you can really feel the power of the mighty Yellowstone as it tumbles over the massive 308-foot waterfall, the tallest in the park.

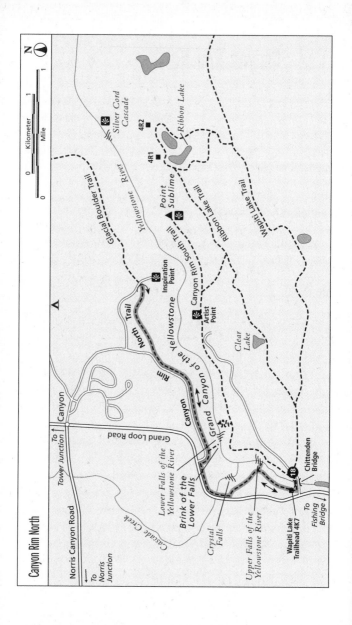

Canyon Rim North

About 0.5 mile down the trail is the side trip to Lookout Point and Red Rock Point. Both give additional views of Lower Falls. Lookout Point is a 50-foot walk, but Red Rock Point requires a steep 0.25-mile drop.

Next at Grandview Point you get one more version of the Lower Falls and Grand Canyon vista. The trail is mostly paved up to this point, but from here to Inspiration Point you hike on a normal unpaved trail. Inspiration Point offers one more perspective of Lower Falls, but it includes the broad sweep of the Grand Canyon in the foreground. The Grand Canyon varies from 1,500 feet to 4,000 feet across and from 750 to 1,200 feet deep. Hot springs in the area weakened the rock and caused extreme erosion below Lower Falls to create the Grand Canyon.

Options: You can hike sections of this trail out and back, or you can leave a vehicle at Inspiration Point to keep from retracing your steps. You can also combine the North Rim and South Rim hikes by leaving a vehicle at Inspiration Point and starting at Artist Point or vice versa.

Side trips: Short side trips to Brink of the Upper Falls, Brink of the Lower Falls, Lookout Point, and Red Rock Point add to this hike. Uncle Tom's Trail on the South Rim is the toughest climb down into the canyon. Red Rock Point is next toughest, followed by Brink of the Lower Falls.

If you take only one of these side trips, Brink of the Lower Falls would probably be your most rewarding choice. At the end of the 0.75-mile trip (one-way) to a concrete platform above the falls, you can't avoid the sensation of being overpowered by nature. The earth (and the platform) seems to quiver as the mighty river plunges over the 308-foot waterfall, the highest waterfall in the park.

The trail is steep (600 feet elevation loss) and includes several sections of stairs. It's not recommended for people with lung or heart problems—but highly recommended for anybody with an average fitness level. An interpretive display on the platform tells the story of how Lower Falls came to be.

19 Ribbon Lake

Starting point: Artist Point Trailhead (4K8)

Distance: 4.0 miles (6.5 kilometers) out and back

Approximate hiking time: 2 to 3 hours

Best months: June through Sept

Maps: Trails Illustrated (Tower/Canyon); Canyon Village USGS quad

Finding the trailhead: Drive south 2.3 miles past Canyon Junction and turn left, crossing the Chittenden Bridge, and go 1 mile until the road terminates at the heavily used Artist Point Viewpoint. The trail starts on the right as you walk down to the viewpoint. Trailhead GPS coordinates: N44° 42.475' / W110° 30.036'

The Hike

The trail from Artist Point is not only a nice day hike but also ideal for someone just getting in to overnight camping and hiking. It's easy, and you're only 2 miles from the trailhead. In addition, Ribbon Lake has a small population of rainbow trout (catch-and-release only with a park fishing permit). You can also have a campfire, and this trip has several possible side trips, one of which can give you a view that rivals that from Artist Point. The trail is in excellent shape the entire way.

At Artist Point, the trail leaves the paved area before the viewpoint and heads to the right (northeast) toward Point Sublime. The trail climbs along the edge of the canyon with an incredible, already sublime view. At 0.5 mile turn right (south) and leave the trail to Sublime Point and head for

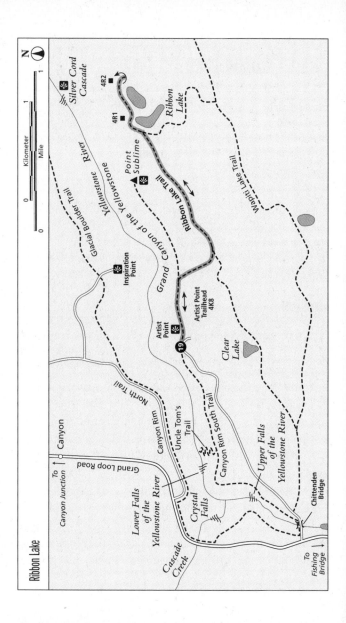

Ribbon Lake

N

Silver Cord Cascade

4R2

4R1

Ribbon Lake

Point Sublime

Ribbon Lake Trail

Yellowstone River

Glacial Boulder Trail

Grand Canyon of the Yellowstone

Inspiration Point

Artist Point Trailhead 4K8

Wapiti Lake Trail

Artist Point

19

Clear Lake

North Trail

Canyon

To
Canyon Junction

Grand Loop Road

Lower Falls of the Yellowstone River

Canyon Rim

Uncle Tom's Trail

Canyon Rim South Trail

Upper Falls of the Yellowstone River

Crystal Falls

Cascade Creek

Chittenden Bridge

To
Fishing Bridge

Kilometer

Mile

0   1

0   1

Ribbon Lake—unless you want to take a side trip to Point Sublime before going to Ribbon Lake.

In less than 0.5 mile is the junction with the trail to Clear Lake, where you turn left (northeast). Some maps may not show this junction.

After the junction the trail is flat and stays in the trees until you reach Ribbon Lake, which is actually two lakes connected by a foot-deep, narrow channel. The smaller lake is surrounded by sedge meadows and may be completely covered with pond lilies.

At Ribbon Lake a spur trail veers left to backcountry campsites 4R1 and 4R2 and to the Silver Cord Cascade overlook. Even if you aren't camping, take the short side trip on this trail for a view of the cascade and the Grand Canyon of the Yellowstone. The cascade is a waterfall off the edge of the canyon. It's eerie to suddenly emerge from the trees and look down at the river hundreds of feet below. The forest offers no clue that you're so close to the edge.

Side trips: Two short, must-see side trips are Point Sublime and the Silver Cord Cascade overlook.

Key Points

0.0　　　　Artist Point Trailhead.

0.5 (0.8)　Point Sublime junction; turn right.

1.0 (1.6)　Junction with trail to Clear Lake; turn left.

2.0 (3.2)　Ribbon Lake Camps 4R1 and 4R2.

4.0 (6.5)　Artist Point Trailhead.

Southwest Region

20 Sentinel Meadows

Starting point: Sentinel Meadows Trailhead (OK6)

Distance: 2.8 miles (4.7 kilometers) out and back

Approximate hiking time: 1.5 to 2 hours

Best Months: June through Sept

Maps: Trails Illustrated (Old Faithful); Lower Geyser Basin USGS quad

Finding the trailhead: Drive 6.1 miles south of Madison Junction or 9.9 miles north of Old Faithful on the Madison–Old Faithful section of the Grand Loop Road. Turn west onto Fountain Flat Drive and park in a parking area about 0.5 mile from the main road. At this point Fountain Flat Drive is barricaded, so you walk on the road for about another 0.25 mile to the official trailhead on your right (west) just after crossing the Firehole River Bridge. Trailhead GPS coordinates: N44° 34.020' / W110° 50.113'

The Hike

The first 0.3 mile of this hike is on the closed section of Fountain Flat Drive. Just before crossing the Firehole River, you go by Ojo Caliente Spring (Spanish for "hot spring"), which is only one of the interesting thermal areas along this trail.

The trail stays in great shape (flat and easy to follow) all the way to the junction with the trail coming in from Imperial Meadows. Watch for bison on the trail and give them a wide berth. Turn around at this junction and retrace your steps to the trailhead.

Options: This hike also makes an easy overnighter for beginning backpackers.

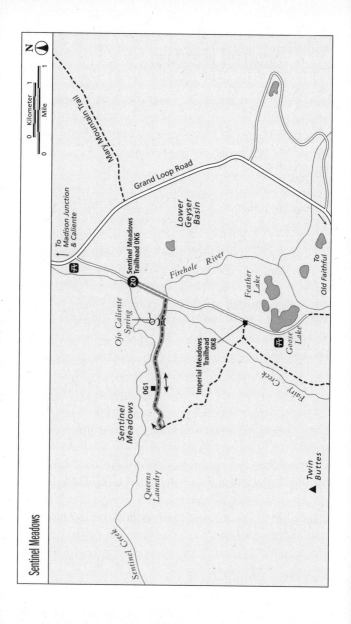

Sentinel Meadows

Key Points

0.0   Sentinel Meadows Trailhead.

0.3 (0.3)   Ojo Caliente Spring.

0.4 (0.5)   Firehole River Bridge and Sentinel Meadows Trailhead.

1.0 (1.6)   OG1.

1.4 (2.4)   Junction with trail from Imperial Meadows Trailhead (OK8); turn right.

2.8 (4.7)   Sentinel Meadows Trailhead.

21 Mystic Falls

Starting point: Biscuit Basin Trailhead (OK4)
Distance: 4.0 mile (6.5 kilometer) lollipop
Approximate hiking time: 2 to 3 hours

Best months: June through Sept
Maps: Yellowstone Association's Old Faithful map/brochure; Trails Illustrated (Old Faithful); Old Faithful USGS quad

Finding the trailhead: Drive 1.8 miles north of Old Faithful or 14.2 miles south of Madison Junction and park in the Biscuit Basin Boardwalk parking area on the west side of the road. Trailhead GPS coordinates: N44° 29.208' / W110° 51.125'

The Hike

Mystic Falls is a popular day-hike destination from Old Faithful and receives heavy use. It's a short, easy hike with incredible views of a cascading, 70-foot waterfall, Biscuit Basin, and the Old Faithful area. In 1988, however, a forest fire burned the forest along most of the route.

From the parking area, cross the Firehole River on a sturdy bridge and follow the Biscuit Basin Boardwalk around to the right until you reach the Little Firehole Meadows Trail at the west end. Watch for this trail heading west off the boardwalk because the junction isn't well marked, and it's easy to miss it and continue on the boardwalk. Go left (west) here, and stay right (west) when you pass the junction with the trail to Summit Lake about 0.25 mile down the trail. Next is the junction with the Mystic Falls loop trail that joins from the right. Stay left for the quickest route to the falls. You can return on the overlook route.

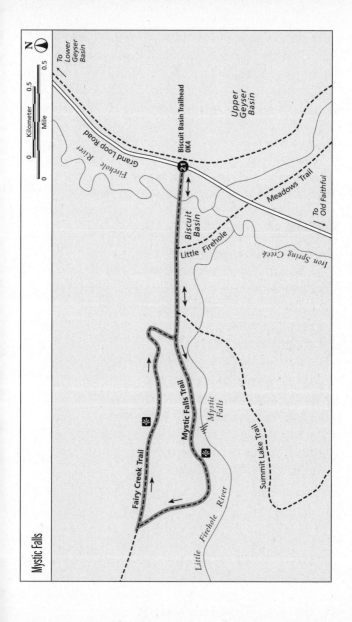

Mystic Falls

At 1.1 miles is Mystic Falls, where the Little Firehole River suddenly leaves the Madison Plateau and drops into Biscuit Basin. Past Mystic Falls the trail climbs abruptly to the junction with the trail from Fairy Creek. Turn right (east) here and hike another 0.25 mile or so to a fenced overlook and sweeping view to the east of Old Faithful, the Firehole River, and the Upper Geyser Basin.

After soaking in the view for a while, continue east of the overlook, dropping steeply, until you rejoin the Mystic Falls Trail. Then retrace your steps to the trailhead.

Key Points

0.0	Biscuit Basin Trailhead.
0.3 (0.5)	Junction with Mystic Falls Trail; turn left.
0.6 (1.0)	Junction with Little Firehole Meadows Trail; turn right.
0.6 (1.0)	Junction with Summit Lake Trail; turn right.
1.2 (1.9)	Mystic Falls.
1.4 (2.3)	Mystic Falls Overlook.
1.7 (2.7)	Junction with Fairy Creek Trail; turn right.
2.5 (4.0)	Upper Geyser Basin Overlook.
3.1 (5.2)	Junction with Mystic Falls Trail; turn right.
3.1 (5.2)	Junction with Summit Lake Trail; turn left.
3.4 (5.5)	Junction with Little Firehole River Trail; turn left.
3.7 (6.0)	Boardwalk; turn left or right.
4.0 (6.5)	Biscuit Basin Trailhead.

22 Fairy Falls

Starting point: Fairy Falls Trailhead (OK5)

Distance: 3.2 miles (5.2 kilometers) out and back

Approximate hiking time: 2 to 3 hours

Best months: June through Sept

Maps: Yellowstone Association's Old Faithful map/brochure; Trails Illustrated (Old Faithful); Old Faithful USGS quad

Finding the trailhead: Drive 5.5 miles south of Madison Junction or 10.5 miles north of Old Faithful and pull into the parking area on the west side of the road, just south of the Grand Prismatic Spring. The trail starts across the bridge on the old Fountain Freight Road, which was recently turned into a trail (also open to bicycles). Trailhead GPS coordinates: N44° 30.981' / W110° 49.963'

The Hike

This is a short, easy hike to a falls more mystic than Mystic Falls.

From the trailhead walk on Fountain Flats Drive as it crosses the Firehole River on a bridge and skirts the west side of the Midway Geyser Basin, with Grand Prismatic Spring off to the right (east). In less than a mile the Fairy Falls Trail turns left (west) off the road. The trail is well traveled and easy to follow as it goes through burnt lodgepole.

Fairy Falls is a delicate, 197-foot waterfall named for its graceful beauty. There's a bridge below the falls, and a short spur trail allows you to get an even closer look at the falls and the deep pool it has carved out.

After enjoying a nice break at the falls, retrace your steps to the trailhead.

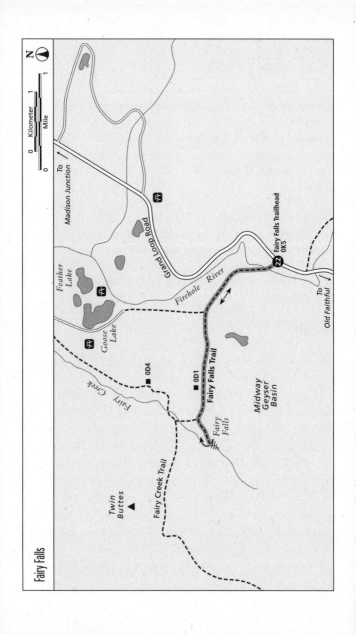

Fairy Falls

Options: There are two other options for getting to Fairy Falls, but this route is the easiest and least complicated.

Key Points

0.0	Fairy Falls Trailhead.
0.8 (1.3)	Junction with Fairy Falls Trail; turn left.
1.4 (2.3)	Spur trail to OD1.
1.6 (2.6)	Fairy Falls.
3.2 (5.2)	Fairy Falls Trailhead.

23 Upper Geyser Basin

Starting point: Old Faithful Visitor Center

Distance: Varies from 1.5 (2.4 kilometer) to 5.0 mile (8.1 kilometer) loop, depending on which loop you hike.

Approximate hiking time: 2 to 3 hours

Best months: June through Sept

Maps: Yellowstone Association's Old Faithful map/brochure; Trails Illustrated (Old Faithful); Old Faithful USGS quad

Finding the trailhead: Drive 16 miles south of Madison Junction or 17 miles west of West Thumb and take the Old Faithful exit. Follow the signs to the visitor center. Trailhead GPS coordinates: N44° 27.535' / W110° 49.646'

The Hike

When you hear people talking about day hiking in Yellowstone, they usually talk about geysers and other thermal areas, and they're probably talking about this hike. This trail goes by an almost unimaginable number of fascinating thermal features. But don't expect to be alone in the wilderness. This may also be the most heavily used trail in the park.

Before starting, go to the visitor center and buy a copy of the well-done brochure and map of the area published by The Yellowstone Association. This brochure is much better than any other map of the area.

Unlike most other hikes, this loop offers several options in length to suit your physical ability and mood of the day. Also, much of the trail is on boardwalks and paved walkways accessible to wheelchairs. The trail and walkway on the south side of the Firehole River is open to bicycles.

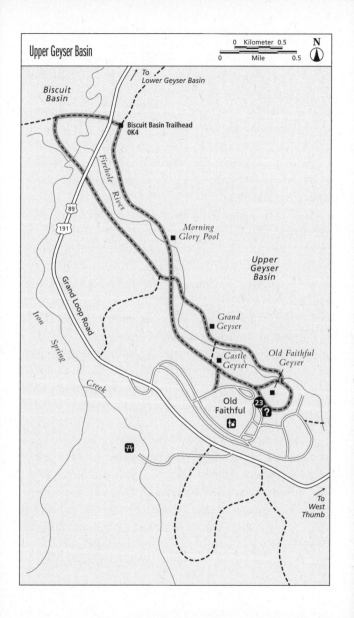

Upper Geyser Basin

0   Kilometer   0.5

0   Mile   0.5

N

Biscuit
Basin

To
Lower Geyser Basin

Biscuit Basin Trailhead
OK4

Firehole River

89
191

Morning
Glory Pool

Upper
Geyser
Basin

Grand Loop Road

Iron

Spring

Creek

Grand
Geyser

Castle
Geyser

Old Faithful
Geyser

Old
Faithful

23
?

To
West
Thumb

The longest route is the Geyser Hill Loop and goes from the visitor center to the Biscuit Basin Trailhead, along the Grand Loop Road for less than 0.25 mile and then back on the other side of the Firehole River. This long route includes about 2.0 miles of regular trails in addition to the boardwalks and walkways.

You can shorten the loop by crossing over the Firehole River on bridges near the Morning Glory Pool (2.8-mile trip) or Grand Geyser or Castle Geyser (1.4-mile loop). Adding the Geyser Hill loop lengthens the trip by 1.3 miles.

All Upper Geyser Basin hikes start out with a bang—the eruption of Old Faithful, which isn't quite as faithful as in past decades. It now erupts on a varied schedule, roughly about 90 minutes or less, but more frequently than any other big geyser. You can view this famous phenomenon from benches in front of the visitor center, or, if you have time, you can get a more distant view from Geyser Hill—or, if you time your hike correctly, both.

It pays to study the map carefully before taking off. The entire trip is on superb trails, walkways, or boardwalks. Even the trip up to the Geyser Hill Viewpoint is in excellent shape with well-planned switchbacks, making the small climb seem easy.

Regardless of how much of the area you choose to hike, set aside much more time than you would normally allow for a hike of this length. Take your time and enjoy it all. The NPS has provided an incredible educational experience with frequent interpretive signs, brochures, and guided tours. Interpretive rangers normally hike the area and can answer your questions. If you're interested in a ranger-led tour, inquire at the visitor center for the schedule.

24 Lone Star Geyser

Starting point: Lone Star Trailhead (OK1)

Distance: 4.6 miles (7.4 kilometers) out and back with loop option

Approximate hiking time: 2.5 to 3.5 hours

Best months: July through Sept

Maps: Trails Illustrated (Old Faithful); Old Faithful USGS quad

Finding the trailhead: Drive 1.9 miles east of the Old Faithful interchange or 15.4 miles west of West Thumb and park at the Lone Star Trailhead on the south side of the road. Trailhead GPS coordinates: N44° 26.673' / W110° 48.264'

The Hike

This is a fairly level hike to a well-known and heavily visited geyser. Lone Star Geyser is so popular that the National Park Service (NPS) has paved the trail and opened it to mountain bikers. Even though you might see a few bikers and more than a few hikers on this trail, it's still a pleasant hike along the Upper Firehole River. About 0.5 mile before the geyser stay right (south) at the junction with the Spring Creek Trail, continuing on the paved path. The pavement ends about 100 feet before the geyser and is blocked by downed trees to discourage bicycle traffic beyond this point.

Lone Star Geyser was named for its isolated location (5 miles south of Old Faithful with no other geysers in the neighborhood). The name has nothing to do with Texas, the Lone Star State. It erupts 30 to 50 feet every two to three hours or so for about ten to fifteen minutes. Gurgling sounds come from the geyser's large cone between eruptions.

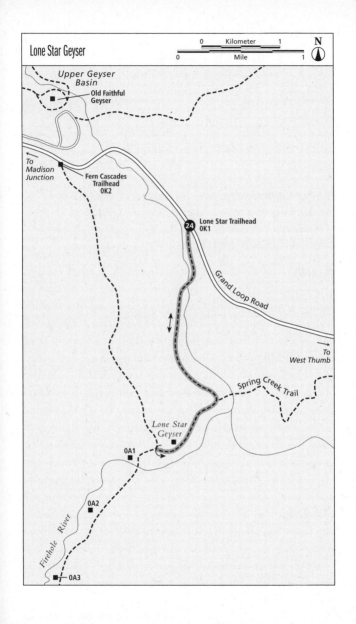

Lone Star Geyser

Upper Geyser Basin

Old Faithful Geyser

To Madison Junction

Fern Cascades Trailhead 0K2

Lone Star Trailhead 0K1

24

Grand Loop Road

To West Thumb

Spring Creek Trail

Lone Star Geyser

0A1

0A2

Firehole River

0A3

0 Kilometer 1

0 Mile 1

N

Options: If you don't want to hike on a paved trail with mountain bikers, you can hike to Lone Star Geyser out and back from Howard Eaton Trailhead (OK2), which is about 1.7 miles north of the Lone Star Trailhead.

You can also start this hike at Howard Eaton Trailhead (OK2) and come out at Lone Star Trailhead or vice versa. This requires two vehicles or a 1.7-mile walk on the highway to get back to your vehicle. Total distance of the loop is 7.2 miles.

25 Beula Lake

Starting point: East end of
Grassy Reservoir
Distance: 5.0 miles (8 kilome-
ters) out and back
Approximate hiking time: 3 to
4 hours

Best months: July through Sept
Maps: Trails Illustrated (Old
Faithful); Grassy Lake Reservoir
USGS quad

Finding the trailhead: Drive 10 miles west of Flagg Ranch (2
miles south of the park on US 287) on a mostly unpaved road to
Grassy Lake Reservoir. The trailhead is not marked, but it's a steep
pullout on the north side of the road just as you reach the reservoir.
Trailhead GPS coordinates: N44° 07.517' / W110° 47.199'

The Hike

From the trailhead the trail gradually climbs over a small
ridge and drops to Beula Lake. The trail is in superb condition the entire way. It goes though partly burned forest, but
the lakeshore itself has not been burned. This is a good hike
to observe how nature recovers from forest fires.

About 0.5 mile from the trailhead, the trail reaches the
park boundary and crosses the South Boundary Trail. Go
straight (north) to Beula Lake.

Beula Lake (named after a mystical land of sunshine and
delight) is a fairly large lake (107 acres) with two designated
campsites. Lily pads grow on the south end, and it hosts
a healthy cutthroat population, making it popular with
anglers.

Options: This hike also makes a nice overnighter for
beginning backpackers or anglers.

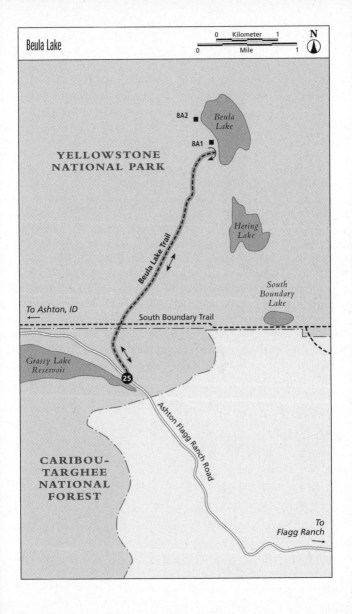

Beula Lake

0   Kilometer   1

0   Mile   1

N

8A2

8A1

Beula
Lake

YELLOWSTONE
NATIONAL PARK

Hering
Lake

South
Boundary
Lake

Beula Lake Trail

To Ashton, ID

South Boundary Trail

Grassy Lake
Reservoir

25

Ashton Flagg Ranch Road

CARIBOU-
TARGHEE
NATIONAL
FOREST

To
Flagg Ranch

Southeast Region

26 Pelican Creek Nature Trail

Starting point: Pelican Nature Trail Trailhead
Distance: 0.5 mile (0.8 kilometer) loop
Approximate hiking time: 1 hour or less

Best months: June through Sept
Maps: Trails Illustrated (Yellowstone Lake); Lake Butte USGS quad

Finding the trailhead: Drive 1.5 miles east of Fishing Bridge Junction and park in the small parking area on the south side of the road, just before leaving the timber and going out into a large meadow along Pelican Creek. Trailhead GPS coordinates: N44° 33.222' / W110° 22.125'

The Hike

This is a short stroll though a marshy area to the shore of Yellowstone Lake and back on a different route. Boardwalks over long stretches of marsh keep your feet dry and allow you to peacefully observe wildflowers. On the lakeshore you can relax on a sandy beach and enjoy views of Mount Sheridan and Stevenson Island, as well as the massiveness of the "inland ocean" itself—all 87,450 acres of it!

The National Park Service (NPS) offers ranger-led nature tours along this trail. Inquire at the Fishing Bridge Visitor Center or the Lake Ranger Station.

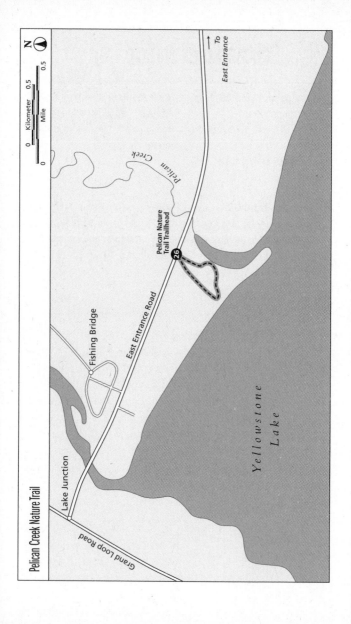

Pelican Creek Nature Trail

N

Kilometer 0.5
0
Mile 0.5
0

Lake Junction

Grand Loop Road

Fishing Bridge

East Entrance Road

Pelican Creek

Pelican Nature
Trail Trailhead

26

To
East Entrance

Yellowstone
Lake

27 Storm Point

Starting point: Storm Point Trail-head by Indian Pond
Distance: 1.5 mile (2.4 kilometer) loop
Approximate hiking time: 1 to 2 hours

Best months: June through Sept
Maps: Trails Illustrated (Yellowstone Lake); Lake Butte USGS quad

Finding the trailhead: Drive 3.1 miles east of Fishing Bridge Junction and park in the small parking area on the south side of the road, about 0.5 mile after crossing Pelican Creek. Trailhead GPS coordinates: N44° 33.568' / W110° 19.666'

The Hike

If you like a ranger-led interpretive hike where you can really learn about the human and natural history of the Yellowstone Lake area, check at the Fishing Bridge Visitor Center or Lake Ranger Station for a schedule of trips on the Storm Point Trail. You can also take the hike anytime you feel the urge without an official guide—and many people do. This is a delightful evening stroll after driving around or working all day. The nearly level trail is in great shape.

The trail starts out by going by the west edge of Indian Pond, a popular bird-watching site in the Lake area. The pond gets its name because it served as a historic camping area for Indian tribes.

After going by the pond, the trail goes through a short section of timber before taking a swing to the right and to Storm Point, a small rocky peninsula that juts out into the

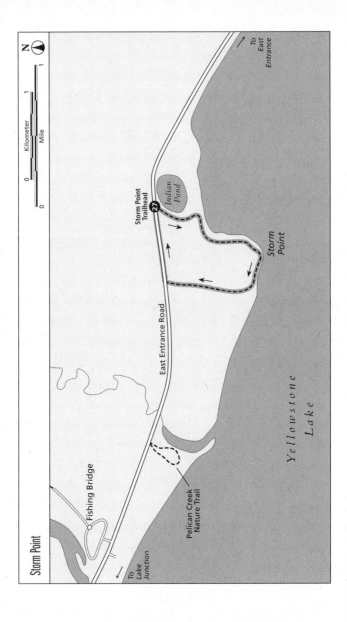

Storm Point

To East
Entrance

N

Indian
Pond

Storm Point Trailhead
27

Storm Point

Yellowstone
Lake

East Entrance Road

Fishing Bridge

Pelican Creek Nature Trail

To Lake Junction

0   Kilometer   1
0   Mile   1

lake, named because it gets seriously whipped by storms moving northeasterly through the park.

After Storm Point the trail follows the lakeshore, offering constant scenic views of the lake for about 0.5 mile before turning right through timber and clouds of mosquitoes (in June and July) back to the highway. The trail breaks out into the same large meadow you started in just before reaching the road. Walk about 0.25 mile along the road back to your vehicle.

28 Natural Bridge

Starting point: Bridge Bay
Marina parking lot
Distance: 2.5 miles (4 kilometers) out and back
Approximate hiking time: 1.5 to
2.5 hours

Best months: July through Sept
Maps: Trails Illustrated (Yellowstone Lake); Lake USGS quad

Finding the trailhead: Drive 2 miles south of Lake on the Lake-West Thumb section of the Grand Loop Road and turn west into the Bridge Bay Marina. Go another 0.4 mile and turn left into the parking lot. Trailhead GPS coordinates: N44° 32.650' / W110° 25.653'

The Hike

You used to be able to drive to Natural Bridge, but the National Park Service (NPS) has converted the trip into a short day hike. This hike is the mirror image of most trails. It starts out as a super trail and gets better instead of worse. You begin on a single-track, go to a double-wide trail, and finish on a paved road.

From the marina parking lot, look for a trail sign and a paved trail heading west toward the campground. Just as you reach the campground, the trail takes a sharp left (south), so be careful not to miss this turn.

From here, walk through unburned forest on an abandoned road along the west side of Bridge Bay for about 0.5 mile to a paved road (now closed to motor vehicles but still open to bicycles). Turn right (west) and follow the road for another 0.5 mile or so until it ends with a little loop, which goes by Natural Bridge.

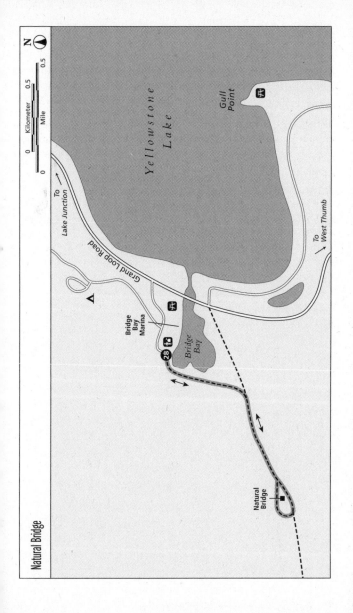

Natural Bridge

Yellowstone Lake

Gull Point

To Lake Junction

Grand Loop Road

Bridge Bay Marina

Bridge Bay

28

Natural Bridge

To West Thumb

N

Kilometer
0   0.5
Mile
0   0.5

An interpretive display at the end of the road explains the story of the Natural Bridge. Bridge Creek flows beneath the ground under the Natural Bridge. Through the centuries, freezing and thawing broke away sections of rock that were carried away by spring runoff, gradually creating the bridge.

There used to be a trail over the bridge, but it was abandoned for fear that the bridge might collapse. Likewise, an early proposal to build a road over the bridge was shelved— or you probably wouldn't be able to see it today.

29 | Elephant Back Mountain

Starting point: Elephant Back Trailhead

Distance: 4.0 mile (6.5 kilometer) lollipop

Approximate hiking time: 2.5 to 3.5 hours

Best months: July through Sept

Maps: Trails Illustrated (Yellowstone Lake); Lake USGS quad

Finding the trailhead: Drive 0.7 mile south of Fishing Bridge or 0.5 mile north of Lake and park at the small parking area on either side of the road. Trailhead GPS coordinates: N44° 34.154' / W110° 33.172'

The Hike

From some viewpoints this forested ridge looked like an elephant's back to early explorers, but you'll have a hard time getting the same impression when climbing up to the top. Nonetheless it's a nice day hike for anybody staying at Fishing Bridge or Lake, and because of its proximity to these areas, this trail receives heavy use. It also receives heavy maintenance and is in excellent shape and double wide most of the way.

The trail goes through unburned timber the entire way. About halfway up the hill, go left or right on the loop trail. Go either way with no added difficulty and take the other route on the way down. The right fork is the most gradual but longest route to the top, but well-designed switchbacks make the 800-foot climb seem fairly easy whichever fork you choose.

From the viewpoint on top enjoy a panoramic view of "the inland ocean," Yellowstone Lake, and Stevenson Island and the massive Pelican Valley.

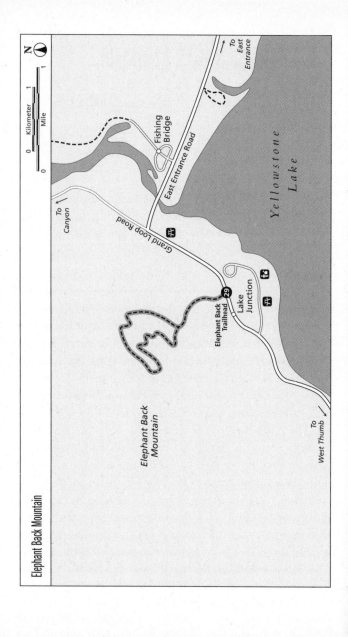

Elephant Back Mountain

N

0 Kilometer 1
0 Mile 1

To
Canyon

Fishing
Bridge

East Entrance Road

Grand Loop Road

To
East
Entrance

Yellowstone Lake

Elephant Back
Trailhead

29

Lake
Junction

Elephant Back
Mountain

To
West Thumb

30 Riddle Lake

Starting point: Riddle Lake Trailhead (7K3)

Distance: 4.6 miles (7.4 kilometers) out and back

Approximate hiking time: 3 hours

Best months: July 15 through Sept

Maps: Trails Illustrated (Yellowstone Lake); Mount Sheridan USGS quad

Finding the trailhead: Drive 4.1 miles south of West Thumb and turn into the parking area on the east side of the road. Trailhead GPS coordinates: N44° 21.504' / W110° 34.907'

The Hike

This ranks as one of the easiest hikes to a backcountry lake in the park. It's just more than 2 miles and flat as a pool table—even though you hike over the Continental Divide!

The trail is in great shape and passes through unburned forest and past several small meadows. Some of the meadows stay marshy until late July, so you might get your feet wet. Some small stream crossings have footbridges; some don't.

Watch for elk and moose in the meadows—and for bears. The area is a key bear-management area, which means it's closed until July 15.

Riddle Lake gets its name because early on in the park's history, it was believed to be a "two-ocean lake" sitting right on the Continental Divide with outlets flowing both east and west. But this was only an early mapping error. The lake is actually about 2 miles east of the Divide, which is near the trailhead.

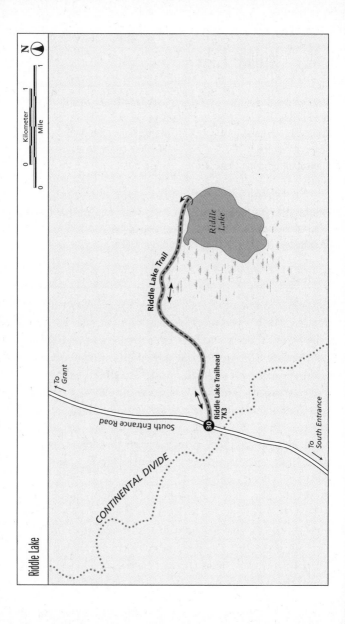

Riddle Lake

The 274-acre lake also has a large marshy meadow on its southwest corner, and in late summer lily pads float on the surface. Cutthroats swim up Solution Creek from Yellowstone Lake to Riddle Lake.

The trail goes along the north edge of the lake to a small beach where it officially ends. You get a great view of the Red Mountains from the lake.

Preserving Yellowstone

The Yellowstone Association is a nonprofit organization founded in 1933 to assist with educational, historical, and scientific programs for the benefit of Yellowstone National Park and its visitors. Through the years the association has raised millions of dollars to help preserve Yellowstone and supplement the park's educational programs.

The association operates bookstores in all park visitor centers and information stations with the proceeds from sales of books, maps, posters, and videos going to fund interpretive programs and exhibits for visitors as well as for research projects and equipment. The association also sponsors the Yellowstone Institute, an in-depth educational program for the public.

You can help preserve the park by becoming a member of The Yellowstone Association. Membership benefits include a newsletter, a subscription to the park newspaper, a discount on books, maps, and videos, and a discount on Yellowstone Institute tuition. All memberships or donations are tax deductible.

To become a member or get more information on The Yellowstone Association, write The Yellowstone Association, P.O. Box 117, Yellowstone National Park, WY 82190; (406) 848-2400; or visit www.yellowstoneassociation.org. To order books, maps, DVDs, and CDs, call the association, visit their website, or stop at any visitor center in the park.

About the Author

Bill Schneider has spent forty years hiking trails all across America. During college in the mid-1960s, he worked on a trail crew in Glacier National Park and became a hiking addict. He spent the 1970s publishing *Montana Outdoors* magazine for the Montana Department of Fish, Wildlife & Parks while covering as many miles of trails as possible on weekends and holidays. In 1979 Bill and his partner, Mike Sample, founded Falcon Publishing. Since then he has written twenty books and hundreds of magazine articles on wildlife, outdoor recreation, and conservation issues. Bill has also taught classes on bicycling, backpacking, zero-impact camping, and hiking in bear country for the Yellowstone Institute, a nonprofit educational organization in Yellowstone National Park.

In 2000 Bill retired from his position as president of Falcon Publishing (now an imprint of The Rowman & Littlefield Publishing Group, Inc.) after it had grown into the premier publisher of outdoor recreation guidebooks, with more than 800 titles in print. He now lives in Helena, Montana, with his wife, Marnie, and works as a publishing consultant, freelance writer, and travel and outdoor editor for *NewWest.net,* a regional online magazine. For more details, go to www.billschneider.net.